Geometry of the Restless Herd

Geometry of the Restless Herd

SOPHIE CABOT BLACK

COPPER CANYON PRESS

PORT TOWNSEND, WASHINGTON

Cover art: Maxfield Frederick Parrish, *The Young King of the Black Isles,* 1929.
Copyright © 2023 Maxfield Parrish Family, LLC. Licensed by VAGA at Artists
Rights Society (ARS), NY. Image courtesy of Mouseion Archives/Alamy.

Copper Canyon Press is in residence at Fort Worden State Park
in Port Townsend, Washington, under the auspices of Centrum.
Centrum is a gathering place for artists and creative thinkers
from around the world, students of all ages and backgrounds,
and audiences seeking extraordinary cultural enrichment.

LIBRARY OF CONGRESS CATALOGING-IN-PUBLICATION DATA
Names: Black, Sophie Cabot, author.
Title: Geometry of the restless herd / Sophie Cabot Black.
Description: Port Townsend, Washington : Copper Canyon Press, 2024. |
   Summary: "A collection of poems by Sophie Cabot Black"— Provided
   by publisher.
Identifiers: LCCN 2023052770 (print) | LCCN 2023052771 (ebook) |
   ISBN 9781556596926 (paperback) | ISBN 9781619322998 (epub)
Subjects: LCGFT: Poetry.
Classification: LCC PS3552.L34133 G46 2024 (print) |
   LCC PS3552.L34133 (ebook) | DDC 811/.54—dc23/eng/20231121
LC record available at https://lccn.loc.gov/2023052770
LC ebook record available at https://lccn.loc.gov/2023052771

9 8 7 6 5 4 3 2 FIRST PRINTING

COPPER CANYON PRESS
Post Office Box 271
Port Townsend, Washington 98368
WWW.COPPERCANYONPRESS.ORG

MIX
Paper | Supporting
responsible forestry
FSC
www.fsc.org   FSC® C008955

For Lucie Brock-Broido

and for Fiona and Roan Isabel

in the life of the wolf

is the death of the lamb

Contents

Coyotes   3

One

And So   7

Democracy Until   8

Paddock   10

To Burn Through Where You Are Not Yet   11

Sanctuary   13

Pitchforks   15

The Last Shall Be First   16

End of Day   18

Trace   19

Almost Aubade   20

Not   21

The Reckoning   22

How to Stay with Sheep   23

Silo   25

Vanity of the Loon   26

Out There   27

She   28

Two

A Few Follow-Up Questions for the Agent   31

The Older Lamb That Spoke   32

Geometry of the Selfish Herd 33

The Pale 34

Bringing In the Stray 36

Already in Your Name 37

Borrower Be 38

Lottery 39

The Handbook of Risk 40

Securing Alpha 43

Mirror 44

How We Speak When We Cannot Speak 45

The Garden 46

In the Time of Leaves 47

Lame 48

Egg 49

Of Use 51

Still Small 52

Loose 53

Salvage 54

Three

Kind Of 57

After a Conversation with Jack Gilbert 58

As We Left the Hell That Was to Be Our Marriage 59

Eschatology as Study of the Next 60

Kitchen Table Math with Lucie 61

Him Again 63

Use Velvet Anyway 64

All of It Meaning 66

From the Book of the Left Behind   68

The Ford   69

Broken Cover   70

Caught   71

Up at the Pass   73

Not to Tremble but Step   74

Keep the Good One   75

Her   77

Foundering   78

Flock Enters Field   79

Being Shepherd   80

Heed the Row   81

Runt   83

Black Swan   84

The Longer Prayer   85

As to Why We Will Not Stop (Making the Hats)   86

Chorus and Anti-Chorus   88

Forage   90

Leaving the Field   92

The Great Undoing   93

Each God Dimming   94

This Now   95

The Place   97

Not Coming Back   99

Acknowledgments   101

About the Author   103

GEOMETRY OF THE RESTLESS HERD

COYOTES

out of the vast
comes one note

which hovers
simply for another

to break into
the first

and neither
end enough to hear

the other
all the way through

the in-between
of where it was

and where it might
have been

ONE

AND SO

The gate left open. By accident,
Or irony, it became the reason,
The excuse. We could not help ourselves

And then we could not help but set out,
Beyond and into our own summer;
Children, harvest, the river mastered,

Town to town grown. And so the gate remained
Swung wide, falling into rot and hinge,
Spindle and chain, until there was only

After. All along we held the seed
Of our leaving. And had already begun
To never remember

What we left: the trail becomes a path
Becomes a road becomes the only way.

DEMOCRACY UNTIL

We believed we knew what made us look up
From the embers. And had been trying
To remember, gathering there. Some of us

Could no longer breathe; some of us
Talked too much or too fast, asked
Too many questions; some not enough.

We stood, and watched our shadows lengthen
As if nothing more was owed. How long had we listened
To the agent, to each other, thinking

We were full of choice. Stake by stake, plot
By plot; the sum would never run out.
My animals, your animals;

My barn, your barn; we were never ready
To know the herd. Each coming from somewhere else
Fills in until whatever might be missing

Does not easily fit. And so the field
Becomes the shape the market requires,
And to set fire just before heading on

Is also to say it does not matter
Which part is played
But that it gets played. We move faster at the end

Understanding we cannot survive
Our own boundary. Tired of being told we are
How we chose, now too much to own; tired

Of the neighbor behind each door, unsure
Of what is said. To bear the far
Now close; to inherit what we did not make

And now must pay for, finished with doing what we need
To get what we want, knowing
It only begins later, after we tell the story;

How blade by blade the grass returns,
Under rut or drought, cut or torn, under light
That cannot keep to itself, and the wheel

Notches again to the top. Any one of us
Can climb down. And whoever checks the axle
And the bolt, only tightens what will again loosen.

PADDOCK

I built the pen to have the wild
Wear out. Rails welded tight; water
Troughed to the brim, to leave overnight

The young, the quarantined, the yet
To be determined. Come morning do not
Expect the known; you were not there,

Let them sort without you; dominion
Never goes well, cannot hold long
The eye of the contained. Approach

With held-out arms then turn as if to leave,
Walk away, but stop again when followed. You and the animal
Having it out, each holding each: the rope

In your hand to do and undo what must be
Gone through: the breakdown, the repair.

TO BURN THROUGH WHERE YOU ARE
NOT YET

Those who take on risk are not those
Who bear it. The sign said to profit

As they do, trade around the one
Particular. Let them credit what you hunt,

Let the future perform. Results are for your
Children anyway; returns can be long

To notice and, when wrong, will right
Unless the drawdown is steep, or of your own

Doing. If only to have known then the now:
The thesis did not revert, never worked;

You did not move
Except to the already—

And as the prodigy breaks from the pack,
Disrupts into the new for just one more

Number on the dial, the deal
Downriver is how you will get paid,

Later, further. Out just beyond
Where you can see. Trust the flow

Is what he said, sort out the secular
As each day reconciles you

Into a morning of leaving. Or at least going;
Coming back at dark to take off your shoes

And ease into that chair. With that glass. Filled
Again. Not yet paid for. All resting

On an infinitesimal wire you have never seen.
Their wire. Their there. You here. Not there.

SANCTUARY

I am not ready
To set you free,

Bound as I am
To each field walked

Out to the border, to
Overgrowth, breath held enough

To hear, or track
Beyond the kitchen light at dusk.

You know nothing
Of the wood, river, or open plain;

A pail at the threshold,
Morning hay thrown:

You, kept in the pasture
Named for the old man,

Who wait amid others
Pressed gate to gate

For the three-sided
Shed, for shelter,

The fence edge gleaned
For any last grass

At the feet of the agent
Who watches how he already paid

For the processed:
The sheared, the lamb. Not about you,

But what you are worth:
What can be got, after,

In return
Without your return.

To climb the narrow holding ramp
One sanctioned end to the other

Is how you will believe
I do my best with what is given

As if refuge,
While from behind come more.

PITCHFORKS

Hang the tines against the wall, keep the aisle
So no horse gets hurt. Leave a barn ready, tools
Quick to find. Each animal enters led

Then crosstied in case the ram
Runs free, the peacock flies three stories
To stay there, and each cat goes missing. Never be

Without a plan; burned into each handle the name
Of men: G. Young, Wm Haskell, E.L. Yates.
Fork of three points, or six, or the many, enough

To lift out the worst, leave the useful. You work
As if to leave no trace, no dung or straw-rot on floorboards
   trod and pissed—
Still you cannot get it out, lime and ash will not

Take it out—in your hand the well-turned end, the heft
Which trembles with yet more of how to keep going.

THE LAST SHALL BE FIRST

I thought the field the answer, the sheep
A question. Everyone wants to be near,

To manage the animal, the range
Of the easily lost. To walk beside

Whatever you believe needs you, unclear
Stretches of weather, another version of wolf close by.

    *

Leaving the valley, not a word
Was said. The guide insisted the meadow

Cannot be seen from below
Until the trees open, until

You are in it. Up where once was fire,
Or rolled away stone by stone, field stays field.

    *

And where sheep graze without reply, I sit,
My boots unlaced, the dog and truck ahead

Without me. A wet nose moves in, then another
In my palm; the given names will soon be the sound

Of what I do. By dusk the fold steadies,
Returns, if I wait, still, and enough.

    *

No ground left untouched. Where virgin begins
Much argued; the fire dies

Merely to come back again. Cold
Sets in and our bottles pack out

As if we never were. Once, the herd knew
Their way without us; now homeward

Must be mastered. With one word I turn the dog
Who turns the sheep. And watch

For the bellwether; he who keeps behind is the one
To put forward. Always last to enter, now first: he

Who did not know he could and does not yet
See the rise and fall of small made large.

END OF DAY

Your boot, faithful
In the spent grass. A pony

Under birches;
The last barn window

Churches the light
As if you decided

To try again
But held your tongue. Fescue

And timothy at last
Laid down, a path

Of old gold
Along which stragglers hurry

As the horse looks up
To weigh the distance,

The one tree
To say: here, here

Is where it must happen.

TRACE

in the abandonment of day
is the color of what you meant

in the leaf turn of one rough wind
is the weep of girdled bark

in the life of the wolf
is the death of the lamb

in what I heard you say
is what will be repeated

in the bird who sleeps
is the air holding breath

in what you do to me
is what I thought I'd never do

ALMOST AUBADE

too many cocks
and she cannot sleep

who came first
now lost

in the squall of each
hour as wrong hour

headlights
which then reverse

mistaken in the scatter
of rain and wind

and the old goat wails
a kingdom unto himself

and the newly born
clamor toward any sound not theirs—

so much cannot be fixed—
the list beside the bed

as if
to begin again

to undo the night
each morning

NOT

that you are unloved
but that you love
and must decide which

to remember; tracks left
in the field, a language
of going away or coming back—

and to look up
from the single mind,
to let untangle

the far-off snow
from sky
until no longer

held as alibi
is also where birds
find agreement

strung along branches
each with their own song
for the other:

to sing even so—
how to hold the already
as the not yet

THE RECKONING

The land ran out. Each year I was more
Upon my neighbor, even with the boundary;
The iron post angled, the tumbled rock

Piled as notice, as how to be between us.
Be fruitful said the old wire, multiply
Right up to here. But it isn't trespass

If the sign grew hidden, the covenant of blue-marked
Trees fallen, storm after storm. I do not want him to tell me
Who I am; I will walk right into his wood

Through to the one field that keeps asking
For me. A meadow that peeks between two white birches
Bending like a bower. Desire begun exactly

With what it has not; how I am bound
By him, and by what he does not want from me.

HOW TO STAY WITH SHEEP

Tired of explaining why. Someone said
To reconcile the sheep, change the sheep. Over

And over they mouth the same ground; the herd
Somewhat listen but still hurry the bend

In shadow. To convey the whole, move one
By one to keep them from what they want.

   *

Beware the old gate: when open, cannot be closed
Until all are through. The hungry pour out

To find the other side
Ruthless in new grass. Loosened onto plenty

Some will be made lame by much, carrying
On their backs the yield bred for.

   *

Lamb what you can. Watch those who avoid muster,
Walk among them often. Small but deft steps. Get

Under each animal to check for blood or scar or
Gone tuft. Work the edge to lay the scent

So the dog will not run off. Let how to winter through
Be permission to die come spring.

   *

And as the outline shifts, look away enough to see
Anything you can against the night. Simple

This vigil, keeping close, your voice
Stitching the dark. The ram bangs

The slatted pen, will not revise;
Each unencumbered sheep settles into her grief.

                 *

Know the firstborn of the yet unmarked. He will use the beginning
Of what you understand for the rest

Of the season; pain is to remember
That it goes on, viable. The task is to raise

Without promise, tend without forecast.
And to hold the supposed stars, too far

To be of use, as shown. The sky does not ask
And the sheep do not look up from grass and

The compass does what it does which is nothing
But find itself. Stay with the last until clear.

SILO

Whoever is the one to ladder up
Never has to say why: the sky his,
And in his climb keeps the necessary close

As below we appear useless. We auger the heart
Of the sealed-off pit, check each step;
What might go wrong before it does,

Work the edge from the inside, the lowest
Door to open last. What does he already know
Looking down to find the pattern, the mistake,

In bad rain, in sudden mud or winter sun—I cannot tell
What I need to tell; us, still in our noise, whine
Of motor upon motor, and his arm waving in shortcut

Which never waits for our answer; each day time
Paid out by our churn, our small corrections.

VANITY OF THE LOON

in the last listen
of summer, the sun

almost done,
a single bird

on the ocean
brings her glistening heart,

pulls all of it
behind;

the entire
taken up by her

one thread until
nothing is beyond

OUT THERE

I thought I built upon a point where none
Had built before. No cellar hole, no dump of glass,
No stair. Like a sudden king

Who makes himself the story in the want
Of one sacred thing. What was wrought
To get all into view with no human yet here,

So the map said. The eagle drops his feathers,
The cormorant lifts herself into a cross
To dry against the wind, the heron

Crackles at the moon. It is a big water
To see without knowing. A large situation
To be in. I dug and dug until nothing but mud:

I went until I was the end, to bring you here,
Make you look. I cannot be alone without you.

SHE

leaned in
to whisper

until you could
no more,

until you threw
her out. Now

what she knows
wakes you up each day.

TWO

A FEW FOLLOW-UP QUESTIONS
FOR THE AGENT

So what does return look like

And how can you be that good

How do you measure risk

And when have you been wrong

What are the benchmarks

By which you get paid

When did you begin

Who came before me

Who else am I in with

When is it worth my cost

How to know when done

When do I redeem

How to tell you

From what happens anyway

Or how much is made

Without you

THE OLDER LAMB THAT SPOKE

That you would be good to me
Should be good enough. Waiting for dawn

To shear; I have tried but cannot see
Myself, the shape, the pattern I make;

Wherever you put your mark
I am in my way. Not everything

Can be solved. To become certain
You have killed much. The paddock keeps

The outside out; the side door of the barn
Left open where men hold up

The bag of the shorn, move off the one knee,
Away from the quick kick of the risen.

GEOMETRY OF THE SELFISH HERD

To reduce the one being gone for, go
Unremarkable. To be mistaken
For another might be to survive:

Fold in, swerve, better close by,
Better dense with others to turn the needed
Margin in fields outspread

With enterprise. All domains end
In a state of danger and whoever falls
Becomes obstacle; options

Overstated, exits obscured, and the gap
Repairs and in that convergence
We do not finish, ever; we figure

Ourselves as encircled circling, the rules begin
Simple as we steer, pass each other
Or not, and into vortex or arrow or even as new

We form the form as we form,
Move to the nearest
Neighbor in a brace of what might come,

Use his or her angle without asking
Where we head; it is too much to remain
In the clear of anywhere without

Your own kind. We do not move
For freedom, we who fill in, ceaseless. Rather
To be where nowhere is left to choose.

THE PALE

Maybe I find what isn't
there; what the mind can do

does not serve: now, here,
ever, and so the outline moves;

night asks for it,
a night gotten through

where I could not see
until some small morning

of breath, hoof, and blood
as the ewe refuses

to rely
on my vigilance: the watcher,

the watched,
and what comes between—

in the left grass
of winter she sleeps

under a bush,
the hush

stitches itself
to itself

and strict the moon
who would only

send back
what she was given.

BRINGING IN THE STRAY

And so the left-alone shows up. Handle
What first appears; to approach, soften
The gaze, use the gap to know your range,

The regret you can endure, a circling
Back into the dust you raised. Do not focus
On the visible; you will slide

Until one side skews the other. How easy the ruin
By the particular. As where you did not go
Ends up as what you wanted. And what you did not do

Gone over, used, used again. Even
With no witness to how you held out
For any kind of return, even if

You make it relevant, the past is only
The tail where you and your grip once were.

ALREADY IN YOUR NAME

Even now your agent ventures the market
Wary of the restless; an untucked
Hoof, a dry mouth, twitching flank. The alley

Narrows as he notes the awake, counts
The unclaimed, the newly delivered. Row by row
He examines each shoulder, each stifle,

In his coat the invoice: yes, he comes
This time more specific; he looks for those
Who look for him, who wait by each stall

As he picks up each hoof, two fingers at the spine
Searching for the one bone carried through
Unchanging and without end, to mark out

As proof of why not go further. And does not understand
We asked only for a sign, not he himself, not him.

BORROWER BE

where the herd is not yet
is where to hedge

this one
could be the one

as the cards
fill with each bid

back and forth
the untethered

spreads, current
value called out

and those who lose
do not look up—

the streak shot down,
each bet undone

by one too many
on the never-seen, and

what you get to choose
is how to call it

LOTTERY

Not for the first time did we line up
Behind others; to be near and capable
And far enough from zero,

Stepping forward to darken each circle
With a plan. In the child's pocket a list of
Our dead luck: birthdays, telephones, addresses

Kept, numbers used again and again
To pick the row, decide upon our column, us
Against the draw. The law of largest outcome

Lays out the more we put in the more
We arrive. I do not want to rely
On what I forgot to ask. We walk out,

Each ball drops: next is forever
And she hurries us along as if we already won.

THE HANDBOOK OF RISK

Do not pull back so far
As to see too much

It never goes away:
Merely moves to another plot

What does not correlate
Is how to choose

If you name it you will lose it
If you have it you don't want it

Excess only known
When up against another

As you cannot manage
What you cannot measure

The strategy used today
Will not exist tomorrow

Cannot be returned
To the bottle

The new will come again
And does not ever end

Seek out who spreads the pain
While somewhere someone pays

We keep saving
What should go away

Absence of evidence
Is not evidence of absence

If you are not what we already have
Then we make you what we need

The alchemy of building one
In order to produce the other

There is always somebody
On the other side

More can happen
Than will happen

Being both long and short
Keeps you in touch with all gods

In any alternative space
Look for a high-water mark

Rushing in at the wrong sign
Rushing out at the wrong sign

It is until it isn't
Every time a different time

Risk begins
When certain of the outcome

So find the gap. Let leverage
Take you as far out as you can bear

Then close in
To watch

How one pivot
Can bring the world

To believe
Itself

Whole
And worthy.

SECURING ALPHA

To generate you, I short you with room
For any decline; any other outcome

My own bad bet. To prove you pure, outside
The ordinary, I solve for some kind of holy:

A fixed point, a solitary lever, and the rest
Of the world I borrowed from. The better man

Would use distress to make his gods
Appear ever more nimble

Amid the velocity,
Even in the long run, as information

Grows louder, moves to the higher-yet
Number. How can everyone be right

Is my good reason for whatever else
To trigger without penalty. Anything might turn

Into a sell. You could increase, and as you do
Significance disappears, grows common;

Not every excess converts
Back to you, even when I thought I had you down.

MIRROR

the near
never near enough

to hold the far
as always next

is also to be
long in looking—

no angle
with which to see

myself in full:
the curve

of who I am and what
I make

only turning
into the almost

of another; one
who requires nothing

and who does not ask
for more and is not

elsewhere while I
am here, never enough

HOW WE SPEAK WHEN WE CANNOT SPEAK

Having put the house in order I went
Up as far as possible, the stair
That cannot deny its noise, in the quiet

Of all fed and watered while you followed
Past the sleeping, the dresser,
The chair. My two wrists taken up by your one

Absolute hand as we lay ourselves down—
Each corner of the bed another reason
To wheel round; the curtain, the sheets, the breadth

Moves like a lost dog between us; two wolves
Who watch each other as if back
From some disaster and have come to know

How it might be with the other; each
On opposite ridges panting: if you will, I will.

THE GARDEN

Even by the gate we could not see
The rows. Only gone stalks, the paving stones
Upturned, the reach of wild cherry, beech, and ash

Over the rusted post as if to claim whatever rises
As their own. Who moves first decides:
Clear the root, the withered stem, the slash

To burn next season. Stakes of names
And faded packets piled, cast out
By the entrance as the plow waits

For us to make sense of each original
Harrow, tamp, or hardened mound. This year
Will be better; the mole and crow each to their corner

As the horse turns to watch you deep in the dirt
To start with the one good and simple seed.

IN THE TIME OF LEAVES

No longer could we find the snake;
The lake revised back into mud, ledge, and lichen.
A clear sky, remorse, and no track found—

Loss cracked underfoot, trees bared,
Their limbs to later let in stars,
Each fang of light. Let all be peril

Without the choir of thought. Your breath, my hand,
Our walking: the leaf has done its work; above,
Now below. Turning against what bore it,

Then to each other, then to the self. Each leaf,
Intricate with its version, and at our feet.

LAME

Winter. To save anything I might lose
I stack the bales beyond the height of
How to bring them down without breaking

And lock the hatch again before the feed
Unseals. The crippled lamb got in last night,
His stumped forelegs on worn cement

A sound only the rat would hear, waiting for
Contents to spill, and he who was born
Perhaps should not have lived but cannot help

Move the breadth of the almost. What am I
To refuse? He cannot be more clear;
Going as far as possible and still not beyond

The closest pail by morning. I cannot be
Everywhere; I want to be everywhere.

EGG

to leave one
or two behind

is to begin again
the long hunger

of more
than we need—

the fox kills
the lone hen,

his mouth
full of her scream—

the raccoon
tears each one open

to leave the head
aside the neck

and ever so delicately
pull out

each egg, tender
without shell: egg

only wanting
to stay

in the dark
making itself

only enough
to be enough

OF USE

It will be praise
That hauls me up
From muck to land

Across your thigh. Is
This my work? I know
What I can make you

And whenever I turn
To see where you are
You come

To begin where last
You left. What I grew
I grew

Under your hand,
Your voice. So much
Already done

With no guarantee
What comes back
In the sack is yours.

STILL SMALL

What did you feed me other than myself,
Waiting for dawn to tell us apart. I saw
Everything everywhere: how the barn would fall

To mud, the soil take back each nail, oil rags
Dragged under rock and layered leaves, trees
Spindling as the clearing closes. The fox

Runs the wall, the snow; a few sentences of post and rail
Keep us for the night. The wolf makes the flock
Flock; what you have not yet sent

Cannot save us. What did I choose merely to be right;
You think I do not know I die: I know
And this is my waiting. What I saw I saw—

Always that red in the margin, the stitches
Of crows until the gray doves finally begin.

LOOSE

And then one morning, you do not come.
The gate ajar. We pour out to be anywhere
You did not bestow—where did you think

We would go—the trouble you undertook,
Stump by stump, the wrenched rocks, the furrows,
Your count and recount to find the stray,

The curious, the slow return at dusk,
The sound of your rattle. You thought us too much
To be wild; you watched our commotions,

Silent; you knew one of us
Would lead you to the other. Who were you
To divide us? The lamb already unsafe

As you hold the wolf by the ear. Hold
Or let go: you or the small. After which
We forget you ever chose, and turn toward

The chute at the point of your finger,
The tilt of your head. We fill the frame
Believing the more we are, the less we will be

Numbered. And a door left open by the tired
Arm of someone. We come back the same,
Mostly together, to be found, and to be fed.

SALVAGE

To leave behind
An outline, which then
Becomes form. Held up,

It is called beauty
For the ability to contain
What we did not know

We wanted to know.

THREE

KIND OF

Last time I looked
You were
Maybe

Different, maybe
Not. Broken
Is how we talk

About us,
Breaking more
As we go;

Admitting
We started wrong
And then kept

On anyway,
Unable to end
With an ending—

What if
We only want
What we leave,

Believing
It might
Want us back.

AFTER A CONVERSATION WITH JACK GILBERT

One reason I took on the same man twice
Was for each island you said yes to.
Our quarrel old. How the life

Of not having turns into how to have
All of it. Ripe cut melon as it runs
Down stubble, goat on the hillside

Unsure of where to head. The town below
To find wine and oil, the smaller fish
Saved just for you. Not the story but the work

Getting there. You enter the river simply
To cross. I stay by the bank for what
I know. The river changes because men change

Every day. For love done only once. Which is
How to explain that last time, that boat.

AS WE LEFT THE HELL THAT WAS TO
BE OUR MARRIAGE

Yes it was your turn
I wanted

undoing some cosmic
mistake

to be up front
my shoulder by your shoulder

but in the old desire and confusion
of always too late

that sad twist was
my need to know

what? What could I
have known instead

for us, to carry
like a small child

into full sun
across the field to

ours the house
ours the door

the one and
only threshold—

so do not wonder:
when one wonders

it disappears
us both.

ESCHATOLOGY AS STUDY OF THE NEXT

Of the road no more road.
Log and stone carefully piled into meaning
No further. No other animal

Is this specific. To continue
Until done without knowing
Is how you have tried. But also

Without revision; each branch
Broken was to admit nothing,
Leave everything

Behind. And to suddenly believe
You see how this ends and still
Not turn or take anything back.

for Franz Wright

KITCHEN TABLE MATH WITH LUCIE

Let L be the total
of the loss;

make B
probability of

said loss and
negative B

probability
of the gain. The vertical

shows rate of growth;
the horizontal

the leverage. High
are the odds to go

adverse
even

at the sweet spot
as you allocate

where and when
you can. So

as you close
your eyes

and your foot
inches forward—

no edge
but how many times

you have
been done.

HIM AGAIN

He does not transpire; all that impossible blood
Will not add up. Too much for his one body
To return intact; another stone church, another

Awe kept possible by the framework
Of worn thresholds, candled naves, a vault,
An arch, a tower. I watched for the one bird

That would not fly. From here it was a bird;
Up close, gargoyle. And it continues:
An overabundance of nails

Made relic, golden thorns atop a throne,
Linen shreds. And still the two boards wanting to be
Simple as lumber, no more than a single man could carry

Without swerving. We store what we cannot make whole:
He who would spill over into never fitting again
And so everywhere is where we left him.

USE VELVET ANYWAY

You who would not grow up
Lay down atop the blanket in an exactitude
Of will not rise again, the cats scattering

Out into the vestibule, hell-bent
For the marbled lobby. No instruction
Becomes the whole of it. A word or two

Such as velvet gone amok, a girl's worth.
One gun, pamphleted in a basket with the many
Colored pills. You said take the red one,

Practice until ready to go famous.
The holy way is to exit before forced
And to stay is to always be leaving

One thing until tomorrow. Closets to keep the stockpiled
Repeated until safe. Certain poems we promised
To outgrow, patterns begot

By some English tread. Doubly thick the plush cloth
Must be halved, two parts to farewell
At the last, rollered and cut into drape

For the dapple. Not dusk but crimson everywhere;
Peek of handwork just before the gap
Trues the hem and boot. Each tongue neatly laced

To its bed. Velvet, velvet, velvet: that which the earlier poet
Said never to use. *The reader will not be moved*
Was sold to us, the spindle and the hook, the needle

And the foot. The tuft must turn without tremble
Or will not be chosen. Must be woven all
At once or the loom will catch, will snarl

Into a mob of strands. And so at least once
I spelled you. And the dreamt
So far: a bowered nest, a hallowed chair, Cambridge traffic

Of how we woke, no more sheep outside
The window, curtain useless as the letter *L*
On the tablet at the bottom of your purse.

for Lucie Brock-Broido

ALL OF IT MEANING

Statue by statue you moved
The fragments. A field full

Of the broken. A man
And a woman look on. A goat waiting

For the road to clear. Birds
Stir; the horse believes only

In the other horse. So we call the goats
And they come, proof

We know what they want. The soul
Like that, steadfast in its longing:

Being done with love
Floods us with love. Even as

Each lover last leaves. One of whom crossed
To be at your feet, suddenly everything,

Suddenly gone, while on some far island
The other keeps by the cave of worn-down stone.

None of this was wrong. The goat
Climbs around for the altered place

To slip over the wall. The hawk
Refuses to open his beak

Until you leave. One talon holds
The mouse who can only pivot

To consider how you keep
Heading to the same place

To ask the same question
Which becomes beauty itself.

for Linda Gregg

FROM THE BOOK OF THE LEFT BEHIND

But I did not sign on to watch this going,
Who goes. Nor did I neglect, or lie down
With fraud or neighbor, or leave off

At some mistaken door. Nor did I cast your belongings
Out any open window, or pretend
A wound, or embellish, or mislead,

Distinct from broken promises;
Nor did I coerce from another,
Directly anyway. And who was afflicted

When I swore to be true; even in deep
I did not cry or transgress or grow proud
As you blazed around the dark. Did not

Harrow the alone, listen in, set my mouth
Without cause; nor anger
After, by river waiting. Nor did I

Defile the animal, quick was my commitment
And in private; nor did I multiply much,
Or foul the water, or curse the children—

And never did I wonder whom I loved
Enough and never ever will I eat my heart
To merely remember, which is also

To forget, as I vigil from where
None of you come back, abiding
All for the weight of a feather.

THE FORD

We lost when it began to grow
Into after and became the only

Place we knew. How far we have come
To rely on chance: that river

Might have cleared, unspooling
In a wholly other spot,

But when my animal came to drink,
Your animal drank on the facing shore

And when they looked up to see
They saw. And so it begins, the trail

From the seep of mud, from new-fallen trees.
And in the season when the water slows

Each animal comes still closer
To hear, to smell the other breath, to keep

Eye to eye; how the footing is narrow
With crossing, overrun, ground-down.

BROKEN COVER

Do not say you only wounded her
Without following her quaking flank
Into the bush, the stumble

In her step. Whoever witnesses the collapse
In the clearing is to bring her to the barn: her one eye
And cheek-edge flap, a patch of underbelly left

On the wire, ripped open in her resolve
Not to let you get close. How she empties herself
To keep moving, and where she stops to rest

Is how she does not want to be found
As is. And as to yesterday's dream
To hold her head upon your thigh; now

Comes dusk and it takes everything
Not to climb back up the rented stand and sleep.

CAUGHT

The net tightens
Only on itself;

Ever more tangle,
A realm

Going small,
Spent down

By its own
Clamor, the struggle

Its own making.
And so the three men

Waken,
Gather

One by the other,
Under a vault

Of sky
To watch

As the trapped
Turns ever smaller

And that which was
About the caught

Is now about them,
In this clearing,

Closing in,
Deciding

How to bring it
Home to bear.

UP AT THE PASS

On either side drops a waste of plain scrub
And drought-driven earth. At the last rise
To stop just before the descent, pulling over,

Silence. Between the click of metal going cold
And animals moving to higher ground, between
What I left and what you did not do: a stray

Backbone of light. The valley below accommodates
A truck gear by gear on its way, an old mercy
Of sun stains the distance. To lose the route,

Out in such open without switchback
Or station, so far up no tree to blaze, where already
None stay but scurry off any ridge, no longer

Unfolding against your length, must I give you this too—
To find I am not even close.

NOT TO TREMBLE BUT STEP

Taillights again;
The necklace I wear.

I write hard when you leave.
No dire dog, no sound save mine

And a bird that cries
In her underwing sleep

And night not exactly dark
And dark not exactly dark.

You once said we may
Already have been here

And not dead. What I want
Is when it comes—

For us, because of us—
No mark can be found

For when and which field knew
Our worst. We never understood

What the grass wanted,
What we should have given back.

KEEP THE GOOD ONE

Always be leaving said the skillful
Foreman. Walk in as revelation

About to happen and in the approach
Let drop how easy

The replacement. Remain quiet
As they solve and do not ever turn

Your back. Stay close as you go,
Not everything can be known; the truck idles,

Indicators dim, the aisle
Delivering right to the far door. Also:

Packed in too close will cost. They know the signal,
Smell of the previous, the hard stops

Of bone or ledge where the shovel hits; begin
As if you already knew, leave room

And do not look into each face, do not end
Holding nothing but mistake. The information

Stares back at us, the stalls
Full of witness. Everything as next

To last. Each animal alone
Is put with another

Until one is finished, and so on. It is alright
To be this tired, each day not quite fatal,

And at least once they heard their name
Called from every direction.

HER

She took all she knew to the verge
Of the meadow, the farthest pine.
Done with the slither, her tongue

Settling each lamb, their wet foreheads hard against her
For more. Any sleep was to breathe
In their breath, their twitching, while here the trees

Apostle silence, the wind baffles. How to be
Suddenly without use: distant the shed, the loosened grain,
Salt. But to come this far is only to look back

At the shepherd—what binds him: the ready stanchions,
The swept floor, and how he looks, everywhere,
Simply to find her. She who brought forth

Over and over, and out of nothing she could remember,
Now bewildered by what comes from her own mouth.

FOUNDERING

Knee by knee she eats the field;
Cannot stand, crosses however

She can, each hoof flooded
With her own blood

Pounding. To come to the end
Of want is to contain

Your own ruin; she cannot stop,
Cannot take herself out

Of the picture
As I write it all down

To a zero, to start
Over, start better,

And how she grows
Is what I make

To make myself look, make myself see
How far I will go.

FLOCK ENTERS FIELD

To head in while no one watches. No witness,
Nothing to pay back. I was to fill the field,
The stone wall left as outline, the fence

Movable, to arrive finished and without harm.
Prepared for each meadow where you may
Or may not be. The flock eats, happy

To be the truth; I was once the way back
To the barn, the trough, the crib, the pitched roof
That keeps the hay dry; now I conflate everything

With everything and do not do well
With silence. Perhaps I have been too long
And cannot step back without the whole

Coming with me. What was already known
I had to find: the dog, the wolf, the lamb.
And then no further. Longing to be with or be you.

BEING SHEPHERD

I put no name to her, knowing
I would kill her. Read the books again, by flashlight
In the lean-to just over the hill, coyotes

Rushing the bush. In the middle of the season
What happened to the last is where to begin.
Know your lambs well and do not ask;

Do not be the cause of what runs them
Down the slope, and when the sheep
Cry out from the back of the truck,

With that driver who pretends not to hear
The question, remember a name is not
Protection, does not bring forth conditions

Where there were none. You shall fall
Short to remain within that gap,
Owing what you do, owning what you don't—

What will you pay back to have seen
Enough; difficult not becoming bound
To what is left, the lived-through, the waste,

The load that cannot be changed without changing.
You thought you could gather with one hand;
Include, exclude. The herd returns anyway

To rearrange, around bias, around wound,
Around the dead, and will not sort you out
As they reconcile their graze on uneven ground.

HEED THE ROW

Back and forth
I undo the dirt:

a field
covered

by acts of
reversing

makes a gospel
of over and over

as the tractor asks
then turns

to answer. To plow
is to pray

in two directions:
to break

into ground
awakening

then to wheel
round

giving thanks
for whatever rises;

to head up the steep
and down the steep,

to lie careful
on the hill

trying to remember
where the ledges are,

the harrowed soil
left as praise.

RUNT

I am the one the meadow did not keep.
Neither early nor late, nor bitter
Storm nor season, and already vanishing;

For three days at her side I stayed,
I fit my heart to hers; amid those
Who grow to market, I was not to be

Long. Buried as deep as what the next day
May bring, made certain with a pile
Of any nearby stone. My one mother, ready to let go

The smallest, and the smallest goes. Perhaps I was a reckoning
For luck. First I could not stay away
And then I was finished; I looked back only once,

Tail pointed nowhere, morning fog
Not yet lifted as I turn, already gone.

BLACK SWAN

And who among us let him in, finally
Distinct and sudden in the deep-green
Risen last rain? The shoulder blades, his widespread

Wing, which does not fold easily
Given the strength of all that flight. After
Each hard weather or rustle in the reeds

Comes our settle back down, certain we can
Explain the unknown. We privilege ourselves, the first
Landed; grass rearranges, and we decide

What is rare, random, or of danger until we believe
Everything should end in white, even after the descent
Of moon as she retracts her one magnificent arm

From the water each night, done with how
We survive our dread, until the color of daybreak still
Alongside the one who suffers for us all.

THE LONGER PRAYER

Field of silos, of did we keep enough
To keep us through; walk the fence-line where
The middle rail broke, reset the traps

By the manger. Did we pay enough
Attention; should have done with less, put up more,
Learned the ditch, repeated the row, the glare

Of sun in your eyes, again at your back, the undersong
Of the sickle to rise, and lower, the tractor
That still runs. Forgive the mind its winter, its gnaw—

The softening ground waits; the ridge
Where the sky steeples with spire, wind vane, rod
To receive what we cannot handle, in sight

As elsewhere small is the first light
To light, each room becoming many
Houses filled with their own good doings until astonished

You also remain. The unlost birds come back
To crown the trees and do not wonder
How each branch bursts into again, how free fall

Is ever the stars. Come home changed
Or be changed; every harvest will be
Weighed against the still to be done.

AS TO WHY WE WILL NOT STOP
(MAKING THE HATS)

This time it did not begin with the beaver
Instead a little farther up the mountain
Where the sheep we keep each year come through

Winter enough to answer us, enough
For us to shear, deft before the coming storm,
To take away from the body what it did not know

It grew and then astonished each spring to feel
The quickening of the lamb, the heft of
Sudden weight crossing one more patch

Of snow. All with an eye out
For the cougar or some such animal
Of which the DNA is no longer

What it might have been, the coyote now
As part dog part wolf
Already commonplace. We have come to know the truth

As no longer true—the old ways do not work
Against the new. How to reconcile the bear
As she wakes to what we now call ours

And how to prepare for the unforeseen
As we throw each sheep handily on their back
To begin at the belly—fleece to shear,

To wash, and pick, to card, to bale, to weigh,
To the depot where all will be spun, dyed
Into the wool we want, knowing it can be done

Again and again without much death,
For the sheep she rises, shakes herself
Back into where she was before: grass, lamb;

Watches until we have pulled away,
As we head back down the mountain—
And in something like ability, or capacity,

The condition of being human, or female,
Or both, we want to knit this out, into
Dawn light, into a long stream

Of making sense, into where we will go next,
Into skeins of design and colors
Of what blood can mean, pinks

Such as rose or carmine, wanton or nearly red,
Timid or raw, healing or newly born,
Scarlet, blaze, bloom, or shell, or blush,

Like the small fingers of a wakening child,
Each stitch to repeat, purl and dispatch,
To get this done, and into that which

We can call sustainable, so those from behind
Can choose from the many hues; likewise
To walk forward with covered or uncovered heads.

CHORUS AND ANTI-CHORUS

January 21, 2017, Washington, DC

All tragedies contain us
With no beginning
To speak of; each time we talk

Ourselves back into gathering
Another step toward
The finally said

Which does not work for all.
To say to one another
What we believe

Becomes the action, to explain
The story while also being
The story. We are enough

Not as one but as one of many.
We have imagined the places
We will not be moved;

Have given many names
To what we can make—
And the river sings as it flows

Past both sides of the city
As it splits the one
Into two. And he who was to be the hero

Is not the hero
And we who are given so much
To sing must move as if this is not

Interlude or merely disruption
As we sing by the engine
That will not cease, and the bird above the siren

In its unexamined freedom
Lifts even higher
As there is no place left to land.

FORAGE

Out here solving for winter grass, words
Get simpler. Which is how it begins:

Aware that come morning, the missing appear
Or not. You wake into either side of what might

Have been heard, then discarded, and the pasture
Scarcely changed. Before, I could not imagine;

After, I cannot imagine anything else,
Except to keep the small alive. Sheep by sheep fed.

*

There are those who number their lambs
And those who paint theirs blue.

Loss marked down. Loss buttoned in
To a left ear or swipe of red at the haunch; the ram

Quivers himself off each ewe.
In the spindle of muted light the others

Do not look up: the low grass
In a song of rip upon rip, mouth by mouth.

*

All I have loved
I have loved alone. Cold is colder

Even as the North melts into the never
Before. I pay for the remainder of

Who already came; this field worked as far
As any can remember. Eaten down to root

I move from ground to ground
And back again. I move each animal and so move myself.

  *

To be the better shepherd
Is to use the field wherever you go.

Sleep when the fox sleeps; carry on your back
All you have known, in case. Circumstances

Change; words lessen. How far to head
Before looking back. Some say turn around, others

Say not. Sometimes the wind is wrong. I am not
The one to keep this edge of winter, last of nothing.

for Lucie Brock-Broido

LEAVING THE FIELD

I watched you kneel to measure what was
Against what was not. The horse and cow
Rattle the gate as you turn to the road,

Through. Abundance no longer anything
But another day done. Burn the old grasses,
Plow in the remainder, the dusk folds

To an emptied bucket. Each row sown
Was how you would never raise enough
To stop, or get out before you began

To hate what might fail. You will never be
What the field remembers. The latch holds—
Alone in the grief of being

Outside what you have made, and the possible
That lies in whatever green you leave behind.

THE GREAT UNDOING

I could not keep you all. Your happiness
Was never useful, only

To keep you safe. I let you eat
Beyond where you should, I followed you

Until you followed me. What did we ever have
In common; I turned you into strangers

To leave, then could not. Every time I looked
For you, I changed. And so I give you back;

Those nights you waited for the door to open
Kept me brave, heading home; not everything

Can be gathered, and how what you want
Turns into what you kill;

I buried what I could, flung the rest
Into the woods, left the salt behind,

Did most of it all the way through.
And when it went wrong I said *see how wrong you were*

And when it went right I said *see how right I was*
And in the barren field the wolf-tree

Became the only shepherd; the dog
Lifted up her head, then settled back down.

EACH GOD DIMMING

Comes time
And they take you
One by one;

By collar, halter, even
Untied: your noise
Worn out, redundant.

And you will go
With those who knew
How this would end,

And take you
With them.
I did the best

With what I could;
I thought I'd be fine
At the end

Of the book, looking up
To watch each shepherd
Walk away, the rope

Loosening
And you never curious
Where it fastened.

THIS NOW

The child asks why can't we begin again,
Where we want, as we open the book to where
The wheel moves over the hard part and here

Is what I want to say: whatever happens, find
The bean, the one you had in your pocket
All that time—ladle by ladle, stone

By broken stone. Even as you keep it
You must spend it. How can we not do everything
We are capable of, knowing

History lies in the mow, where once we lay down to see
How it was to be animal. And yes, I took the herd
To the end; what I thought horizon, or at least pasture,

Kept opening further, into the arms of
Where I kept going and wherever I sat down.
To stay was to become a tree, a bird,

The rock I fell asleep on; I worked hard
To change the lamb into the needed
Only to find he cannot be outside

What he already has. And so I cannot tell you
Anything the story does not; eventual is the water,
And a seal upon the ledge as the tide turns

Ever higher, stronger; why must we
Finish here, now, even as we both try
To stay awake, as the seal sings her song

Of how we go; us, no more
The miracle we thought we were. On the last page
Someone just wants to be right;

A worry spot appears, a thorn, a vex,
The shiver which does not go away,
Which slips the worn-out piece

To the one place we weren't
Enough; doing, undoing, until done
And without an answer. The child closes

The book. Keep going; ask,
Then ask again. Refuse what you inherit
And do not forget

The contents of your pocket: the bean,
And then the coming rain. Where you are is
Here you are. Love, anyway; love, without use.

THE PLACE

Ahead is a hut. The little house of
Where you were not to go when young. Worn is the road
Of how you passed by, and now the hut

Stands in the clearing like an owl
On the lowest branch watching. Chimney smoke
Proverbs in with dusk, the settling mist

Slowly untangles. May you be enough
To ask. You enter, sit down, chair
And shawl. Much has been given away. No more dog,

With one eye on the blaze, the other
On the door. Certain objects on the table
To remember, until the door is knocked, until you open

And he who waits outside will not come in,
Then does, stooping, the cold yet on the coat
And you trying to get the words in the right order.

NOT COMING BACK

What exactly did you want us
To endure. And after: who will call out beauty
The way we do. Where will you go

For any awe, the fill of it coming
Sudden or slow, planned or not:
Birdsong as sung back, sunrise

As painted. Did you not want
Each retelling? Was that not the way
You put the world to sleep each night, tenderly—

Acknowledgments

"Geometry of the Selfish Herd" adapts its title and much of its physics from W.D. Hamilton's article "Geometry for the Selfish Herd."

Many thanks to the editors of the following publications where these poems originally appeared:

The Academy of American Poets Poem-a-Day: "As to Why We Will Not Stop (Making the Hats)," "Not"

AGNI: "From the Book of the Left Behind"

The American Poetry Review: "Almost Aubade," "Being Shepherd," "The Last Shall Be First"

Conjunctions: "Geometry of the Selfish Herd," "Runt," "Up at the Pass"

Gulf Coast: "Trace," "Use Velvet Anyway"

Mercurius: "Not Coming Back"

The New Criterion: "Paddock"

The New Yorker: "Chorus and Anti-Chorus," "Leaving the Field," "The Longer Prayer," "Silo," "To Burn Through Where You Are Not Yet"

Plume: "The Ford"

Salamander: "Salvage"

The Eloquent Poem: 128 Contemporary Poems and Their Making: "Forage," "The Handbook of Risk" (edited by Elise Paschen, Persea Press)

Leaning toward Light: Poems for Gardens & the Hands That Tend Them: "The Garden" (edited by Tess Taylor, Storey Publishing)

Much gratitude to Michael Wiegers, Ryo Yamaguchi, Claretta Holsey, and everyone else at Copper Canyon Press, for their care and wisdom.

Many thanks to Mark C. Taylor, to whom I am much indebted.

And also to Elise Paschen, and for her invitation to submit an eclogue to her anthology, *The Eloquent Poem: 128 Contemporary Poems and Their Making.*

And of course many thanks to our motley Zoomsbury Group for getting us through: Ricky Ian Gordon, Richard McCann, Nick Flynn, Martin Moran, Pádraig Ó Tuama, Vievee Francis, Michael Klein, and Mark Conway. And my deepest and forever gratitude to Marie Howe, Donna Masini, and Victoria Redel.

Finally, to my family, elder and younger, for all they bring to my doorstep.

About the Author

Sophie Cabot Black is the author of three previous poetry collections: *The Exchange* (2013), *The Descent* (2004), and *The Misunderstanding of Nature* (1994). She lives in New England.

Poetry is vital to language and living. Since 1972, Copper Canyon Press has published extraordinary poetry from around the world to engage the imaginations and intellects of readers, writers, booksellers, librarians, teachers, students, and donors.

WE ARE GRATEFUL FOR THE MAJOR SUPPORT PROVIDED BY:

academy of american poets

OFFICE OF ARTS & CULTURE
SEATTLE

amazon literary partnership

THE PAUL G. ALLEN FAMILY FOUNDATION

CULTURE

Hawthornden Foundation

INGRAM CONTENT GROUP

the point
envision·enact·evolve

Lannan

WASHINGTON STATE ARTS COMMISSION

ART WORKS.
National Endowment for the Arts
arts.gov

The Witter Bynner Foundation for Poetry

TO LEARN MORE ABOUT UNDERWRITING
COPPER CANYON PRESS TITLES,
PLEASE CALL 360-385-4925 EXT. 103

WE ARE GRATEFUL FOR THE MAJOR SUPPORT PROVIDED BY:

Anonymous

Richard Andrews and
    Colleen Chartier

Jill Baker and Jeffrey Bishop

Anne and Geoffrey Barker

Donna Bellew

Will Blythe

John Branch

Diana Broze

John R. Cahill

Sarah Cavanaugh

Keith Cowan and Linda Walsh

Peter Currie

Stephanie Ellis-Smith and
    Douglas Smith

Mimi Gardner Gates

Gull Industries Inc.
    on behalf of William True

Carolyn and Robert Hedin

David and Jane Hibbard

Bruce S. Kahn

Phil Kovacevich and Eric Wechsler

Maureen Lee and Mark Busto

Ellie Mathews and Carl Youngmann
    as The North Press

Larry Mawby and Lois Bahle

Petunia Charitable Fund and
    adviser Elizabeth Hebert

Suzanne Rapp and Mark Hamilton

Adam and Lynn Rauch

Emily and Dan Raymond

Joseph C. Roberts

Cynthia Sears

Kim and Jeff Seely

Tree Swenson

Barbara and Charles Wright

In honor of C.D. Wright,
    from Forrest Gander

Caleb Young as C. Young Creative

The dedicated interns and faithful
    volunteers of Copper Canyon Press

The pressmark for Copper Canyon Press
suggests entrance, connection, and interaction
while holding at its center
an attentive, dynamic space for poetry.

This book is set in Reminga Pro.
Book design by Gopa & Ted2, Inc.
Printed on archival-quality paper.